Discovering Religions

Sikhism

Sue Penney

D1459418

Heinemann Educational Publishers
Halley Court, Jordan Hill, Oxford, OX2 8EJ
Part of Harcourt Education Ltd.

Heinemann is the registered trademark of Harcourt Education Ltd.

First published 1988
Revised edition published 1995

07 06
17 16 15 14 13

British Library Cataloguing in Publication Data
A catalogue record for this book is available from the British Library

10-digit ISBN 0 435304 70 4
13-digit ISBN 978 0 435304 70 6

Designed and typeset by Visual Image
Illustrated by Gecko Limited. Adapted into colour by Visual Image
Produced by Mandarin Offset
Printed in Great Britain by Bath Press Colourbooks

Acknowledgements

Religious Studies consultant: W Owen Cole

Thanks are due to Professor Bakhshish Singh for reading and advising on the manuscript.

The publishers would like to thank the following for permission to reproduce photographs:
Andes Press Agency pp. 11, 21, 28, 44; Mohamed Ansar/Impact Photos p. 23; Circa Photo Library pp. 10, 42, 43; Mary Evans Picture Library p. 25; Sally and Richard Greenhill pp. 9, 36; Robert Harding Picture Library p. 26; Judy Harrison/Format Partners pp. 12 (top), 33, 39; The Hutchison Library pp. 6, 12 (below), 18, 22, 40, 41; Christine Osborne Pictures pp. 13, 14, 32, 34, 35, 38, 46; Ann and Bury Peerless pp. 17, 19, 27, 29, 30, 31; Harjinder Singh Sagoo p. 47; Peter Sanders pp. 15, 45.

The publishers would like to thank Peter Sanders for permission to reproduce the cover photograph.

The publishers have made every effort to trace the copyright holders, but if they have inadvertently overlooked any, they will be pleased to make the necessary arrangements at the first opportunity.

Contents

MAP: where the main religions began

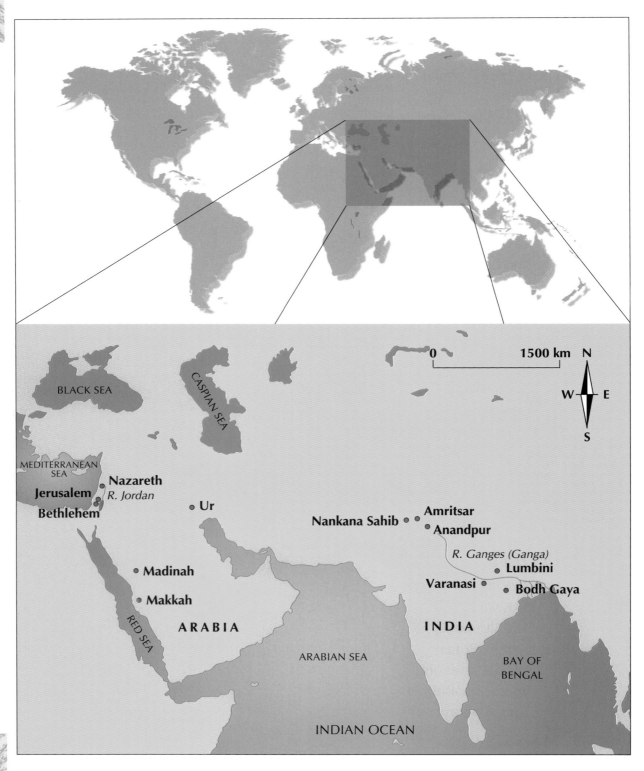

BLACK SEA

CASPIAN SEA

0   1500 km   N

W   E

S

MEDITERRANEAN SEA

Nazareth
R. Jordan

Jerusalem

Bethlehem

Ur

Nankana Sahib   **Amritsar**
Anandpur

R. Ganges (Ganga)

Madinah   **Lumbini**

Varanasi   **Bodh Gaya**

Makkah

RED SEA

ARABIA   INDIA

ARABIAN SEA   BAY OF BENGAL

INDIAN OCEAN

TIMECHART: when the main religions began

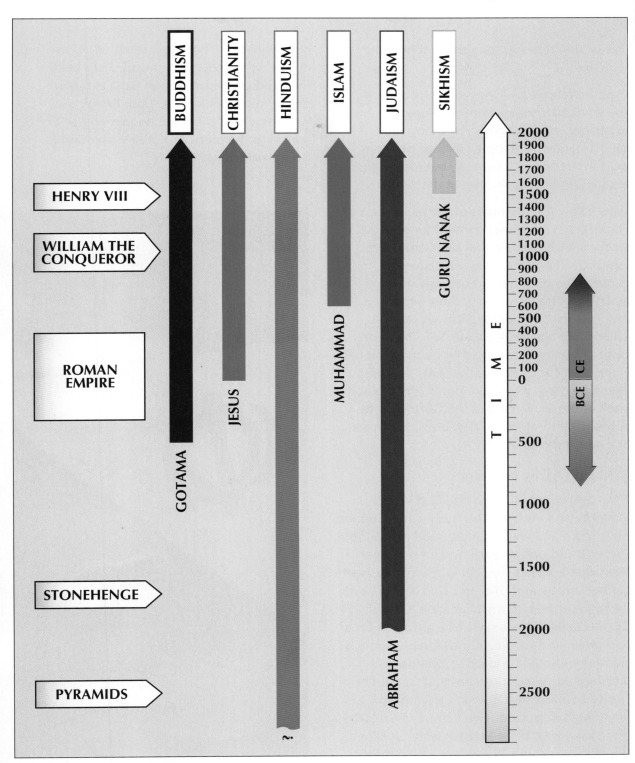

Note about dating systems

In this book dates are not called BC and AD which is the Christian dating system. The letters BCE and CE are used instead. BCE stands for 'Before the Common Era' and CE stands for 'Common Era'. BCE and CE can be used by people of all religions, Christians too. The year numbers are not changed.

Introducing Sikhism

This section tells you something about who Sikhs are.

Sikhs are followers of the religion of Sikhism. The word Sikh comes from the **Punjabi** language, which is spoken by many Sikhs. It means learner or **disciple**. Sikhism began in India in the fifteenth century, but today there are Sikhs in many countries of the world.

Sikhs follow the teachings of **Gurus**. Guru is a title which is often used in India for religious teachers. Sikhs believe that ten Gurus were especially important. They were spiritual guides, who gave human beings God's teachings. These teachings show Sikhs how to live. The first Guru of the Sikhs was a man called Guru Nanak (see page 16). The tenth Guru said that there would be no more human Gurus after him. Instead, the Sikhs' teacher would be their holy book. This is why the holy book of the Sikhs is called the **Guru Granth Sahib**. Granth means a large book. Sahib is a title which shows respect.

What do Sikhs believe?

Sikhs believe that there is one God who is almighty and **eternal**. This means that God was never born and will never die. God made the universe and everything in it, and is present everywhere and in everything. Human beings cannot understand God, but God is good and cares about everything in creation. One of Guru Nanak's hymns says, 'You are our mother and father and we are your children'. God is a spirit who should be loved, prayed to and worshipped. Sikhism teaches that God is the greatest Guru and it is wrong to worship anything except God. Two names which Sikhs often use for God are **Satnam** which means 'eternal reality' and **Waheguru** which means 'wonderful Lord'.

Notice that care has been taken not to use 'he' or 'she' when referring to God. Sikhs believe that God created male and female, but is neither male nor female. Guru Nanak said, 'God is neither a woman nor a man nor a bird' and Sikhs therefore do not describe God as being male or female.

The Sikh symbol

The symbol of the Sikhs

The symbol often used for Sikhism is made up of three parts. On the outside there are two swords. These are to show that Sikhs should serve God by teaching the truth and by fighting for what is right. Between the swords is a circle which reminds them that God is one, and has no beginning and no end. In the centre is a two-edged sword called a **khanda**. This is a symbol of the power of God.

Another symbol which Sikhs often use is made up of letters, which mean 'there is only one God'. These are the first words of the Guru Granth Sahib.

This means 'There is only one God'

New words

Disciple follower of a particular teacher
Eternal lasting for ever
Guru religious teacher (for Sikhs, one of ten religious leaders)
Guru Granth Sahib Sikh holy book
Khanda two-edged sword
Punjabi language spoken by most Sikhs
Waheguru Sikh name for God
Satnam Sikh name for God

Test yourself

What does 'Sikh' mean?

How many Gurus were there?

What's the two-edged sword called?

What are the first words of the Guru Granth Sahib?

Things to do

1 Look at the Sikh symbol in the photograph on the opposite page. Copy it carefully, and label the different parts to explain the symbol's meaning.

2 Who was the first Guru of the Sikhs? Explain why Sikhs believe that the Gurus were so important.

3 Why is the Sikh holy book called the 'Guru' Granth Sahib?

4 What two names do Sikhs often use for God? Explain as carefully as you can what Sikhs believe about God.

5 When and where did Sikhism begin? Look at the map and timechart at the beginning of this book to find out more information.

The five Ks

This section tells you about the special things which Sikhs who are full members of the religion wear to show their faith.

Everyone who is a full member of the Sikh religion should wear five symbols to show that they are Sikhs. These symbols are often called the five Ks, because in the Punjabi language which many Sikhs speak, their names all begin with the letter K. The five Ks were introduced by the tenth Guru, Guru Gobind Singh. Each of them reminds Sikhs of something about their religion.

Kesh

'Kesh' means uncut hair. The Guru said that hair should be allowed to grow naturally. For men, this includes not shaving. At the time of Guru Gobind Singh, some holy men let their hair become tangled and dirty. The Guru said that this was not right. Hair should be allowed to grow, but it should be kept clean and should be combed at least twice a day.

Kangha

The kangha is a small comb. It is worn in the hair, and is used to keep the hair fixed in place. For Sikhs, keeping clean and tidy is part of their religion. Combing their hair reminds them that their lives should be tidy and organized, too.

Kirpan

The kirpan is a sword. It reminds Sikhs that it is their duty to fight against evil. A kirpan should never be used for attacking people. A kirpan may be up to a metre long, but most Sikhs today carry a short sword about 10 cm long. It is usually kept in a special case fixed to a strap over the person's shoulder.

Kara

The kara is a steel bangle worn on the right wrist. At first it was probably broader than the one which Sikhs wear today, and was intended to protect the arm in battle. Today it is worn as

Kesh

Kangha

Kirpan

Kachera

Kara

The five K's

a symbol. The circle reminds Sikhs that God has no beginning and no end, and the steel reminds them of the strength they must have when fighting for what is right.

Kachera

Kachera are short trousers which are worn as underwear. At the time when they were introduced, most people in India wore long, loose clothes. Guru Gobind Singh said that the change in style was a symbol that people were leaving behind old ideas and following better ones. Kachera were also more practical, especially in battle.

The turban

The turban is not one of the five Ks, but many male Sikhs and some female Sikhs wear one. It has become one of the symbols of Sikhism. It is a long piece of cloth which is wound around the head so that it covers it. Turbans help to keep the long hair tidy, but they are also worn because they copy what the Sikh Gurus wore.

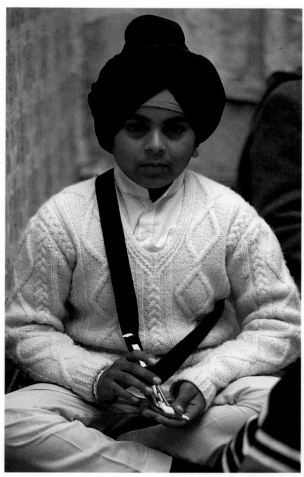

This Sikh boy is wearing a turban and the five Ks

Test yourself

Who introduced the five Ks?

Why are they called the five Ks?

What's a turban?

Things to do

1 How many reasons can you give for why Sikhs wear the five Ks?

2 Draw each of the five Ks. Beside each drawing, write a brief explanation of what it is, and explain why it is a symbol.

3 What are the advantages of wearing symbols that show your religion? Can you think of any disadvantages?

4 Working in pairs, think of as many groups of people as you can who can be recognized by what they wear.

The gurdwara

This section tells you about the Sikh place of worship.

The Sikh place of worship is called the **gurdwara**. This means 'Guru's door' – in other words, a gurdwara is God's house. A gurdwara does not have to be a special building. Especially outside India, gurdwaras may be in ordinary houses or in other buildings. The important thing is not the building, it is the fact that the Guru Granth Sahib, the Sikh holy book, is there.

All gurdwaras have some things in common. There is always a room where the people meet for worship. If the building is large enough, there is also a small room where the Guru Granth Sahib is kept when it is not in the worship room. A kitchen is essential. It is part of Sikh worship that everyone present should be able to share a meal when the service is over. At the entrance to the gurdwara there are separate rooms where men and women can wash their hands and feet, and areas where they can leave their shoes. No-one wears shoes in the worship room. Sikhs are expected not to smoke or drink alcohol, so these things are not allowed in a gurdwara.

Outside the gurdwara

Gurdwaras which are specially built may have a dome and decorations on the outside, but these are not essential. The one thing by which all gurdwaras can be recognized is the flag which flies outside. It is yellow, with the Sikh symbol on it, and is called the **Nishan Sahib**. It always flies above the level of the building.

The worship room

The proper name for the worship room is the diwan hall. It is often decorated with tinsel and small lights. There may be pictures of Guru Nanak and the other Gurus on the walls, although some Sikhs do not approve of this because they think people may begin to worship the pictures. The diwan hall usually has a carpet, but there are no seats. All worshippers sit on the floor, as a sign that everyone is equal. The most important part of the room is the platform at one end. This is called the **takht**, which means throne. The Guru Granth Sahib is placed upon it, on a special stool called a **manji**. The takht is the same sort of throne as a human guru would sit on, and shows that the book is treated with the same respect. In front of the takht is a place where people can leave gifts of food or money.

A gurdwara in Manchester

WORSHIP

A takht

The langar

Sikh services are always followed by a meal which is called the **langar**. Everyone at the service is welcome at the langar, too. It is an important part of Sikh worship which goes back to the days of Guru Nanak. In India at that time, there were strict rules which said that different groups of people should not eat together. Guru Nanak said that being a Sikh was more important than these rules, and the meal became a symbol of the Sikh belief that all people are equal. The food is cooked and served by both men and women, and is given free to everyone. It is paid for by money which people give at the beginning of the service, and by other offerings. The meal is intended to be simple and wholesome, and always consists of dishes which would be eaten in the Punjab, no matter where in the world the gurdwara is. The food is vegetarian, so that people who do not eat meat can still take part.

New words

Gurdwara Sikh place of worship
Langar free meal which ends Sikh services
Manji stool on which the Guru Granth Sahib is placed
Nishan Sahib Sikh flag
Takht 'throne' (for Guru Granth Sahib)

Test yourself

What does 'gurdwara' mean?

What's the Nishan Sahib?

What's the langar?

Things to do

1 What is the most important thing about a gurdwara? How would you recognize a gurdwara?

2 Explain why the Guru Granth Sahib is always placed on a throne.

3 Using the text and picture to help you, write a description of what you would expect to see in a Sikh worship room.

4 Why did the langar begin? Explain why it is such an important part of Sikh worship.

Worship in the gurdwara

This section tells you about how Sikhs worship in the gurdwara.

Sikhs do not have a particular day of worship. Many gurdwaras are open from dawn to sunset every day for people to call in to pray, with services in the morning and evening. In Britain, the main services are usually held on a Sunday, because it is a convenient day for many people. The most important room in a gurdwara is the worship room where Sikhs meet together in the same place as the Guru Granth Sahib. They say that this is like being in front of God.

Any Sikh who is respected by the others may lead the worship in a gurdwara. There is usually one person in each gurdwara whose job is to read from the Guru Granth Sahib and to lead the prayers. This person is called the **granthi**. He or she sits behind the Guru Granth Sahib, facing the rest of the people. Sometimes the granthi waves a **chauri** over the Guru Granth Sahib. This is a special fan made of hair or feathers. It is the same sort of fan which was held over kings in India, and is waved over the Guru Granth Sahib to show the same respect.

Before they go into the worship room, everyone takes off their shoes. They may wash their hands and feet, or may have had a bath at

A Sikh service

home before coming to the gurdwara. Any man who is not wearing a turban covers his head. These things are all to show respect for the Guru Granth Sahib. When they go into the room, the people go to the front and bow or kneel in front of the Guru Granth Sahib. They leave offerings of food or money. As they go to sit down, they are careful never to turn their backs on the Guru Granth Sahib, because this would show a lack of respect. The people sit on the floor to show that everyone is equal, and that the Guru Granth Sahib is the most important thing in the room. It is usual for men and women to sit on opposite sides of the room.

Worship

Services in a gurdwara are usually held in Punjabi, the language spoken by most Sikhs. They may last up to five hours, but they are very relaxed, and people are not expected to stay for the whole time – they may arrive after the beginning, or leave before the end.

Musicians are very important in Sikh services

The Ardas

WORSHIP

The aim of Sikh worship is to give praise to God. Most worship consists of reading and singing of hymns from the Guru Granth Sahib, and from other books like the writings of the Gurus. The singing of the hymns is called **kirtan** and is very important. It is done by musicians called **ragis**, and the people do not always join in the singing. There are talks too, which help to explain the **Scriptures**, or may be about things which affect Sikhs in their lives.

The Ardas

All services end with the **Ardas**, a special prayer which lasts about fifteen minutes. Everyone stands, with one person in front of the rest, facing the Guru Granth Sahib. This person leads the prayer, which reminds everyone to remember God and the ten Gurus, and to pass on the teachings of the Guru Granth Sahib. Prayers are said for Sikhs and all people everywhere, and there may be special prayers for people who are ill or who need prayers for some other reason.

Whilst the Ardas is being said, the **karah parshad** is stirred with a kirpan. Karah parshad is a special 'pudding' which is made of equal quantities of flour, sugar and ghee (specially prepared butter) and mixed in an iron bowl. It is given to everyone who has attended the service, as a symbol that everyone is equal. At the end of the service, everyone shares the langar.

New words

Ardas prayer which ends service
Chauri special fan
Granthi person who leads worship
Karah parshad special food given out at the end of Sikh services
Kirtan singing of hymns from the Guru Granth Sahib
Ragi Sikh musician
Scriptures holy books

Test yourself

What's a chauri?

What's a granthi?

What's a ragi?

Things to do

1 Why do you think Sikhs say that being in front of the Guru Granth Sahib is like being with God?

2 What is karah parshad? Why do Sikhs eat it at the end of services?

3 Explain what the Ardas prayer is. What sort of things do you think might be included in the special prayers with which it ends?

4 If there is one in your area, try to arrange a visit to a gurdwara. If this is not possible, work in small groups to design a building which would be suitable for use as a gurdwara.

The Guru Granth Sahib

This section tells you about the Sikh holy books.

The Guru Granth Sahib

The most important of the Sikh holy books is the Guru Granth Sahib. It was begun by the first Guru, Guru Nanak. He composed hundreds of hymns praising God, and 974 of them are in the Guru Granth Sahib. In 1604 CE the fifth Guru, Guru Arjan, had an official collection of hymns put together. This contained the hymns of Guru Nanak and hymns written by the other Gurus. It also contained hymns written by **Hindu** and **Muslim** holy men. The hymns praise God, and say what God is like. They also include advice about the right way to live. This book is called the Adi Granth, which means 'original book'. Guru Arjan had a special building erected where it could be kept. The original Adi Granth still exists today, and Sikhism is the only religion in the world which still has the first copy of its holy book.

Removing the covers from the Guru Granth Sahib

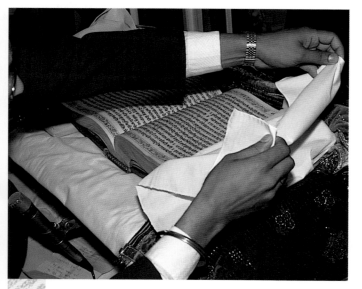

In 1706 CE, the tenth Guru added hymns which had been written by his father, the ninth Guru. This completed the Guru Granth Sahib and, since that date, nothing has been added or taken away from it. For nearly 200 years, copies of it were written out by hand, very carefully so that no mistakes were made. In 1852, the first copy was printed. Sikhs decided that every copy should be exactly the same, and so today every copy of the Guru Granth Sahib has the same number of pages – 1430 – and particular hymns are always to be found on the same page.

Some Sikhs have their own copy of the Guru Granth Sahib at home. They believe that, because it is so important, it should not be placed on a shelf like other books, but should have a room of its own. This room then becomes a gurdwara, because the Guru Granth Sahib is there. For many Sikhs, of course, this is not possible, so instead, most have a smaller book called a **gutka**. This contains the most important hymns and the daily prayers. A gutka, too, is treated with great respect, and is kept wrapped in a cloth when it is not being used. Before reading from it, Sikhs will wash their hands.

The Guru Granth Sahib is used in all Sikh worship, and it takes the most important place in the gurdwara. Weddings are held in front of it, and it is used to help in the naming of babies. When it is open it is kept on the takht, resting on a cloth and three cushions. There is always someone sitting behind it, and it is never left unattended. When it is closed it is carefully covered with special cloths. A Guru Granth Sahib is put away at night in a special ceremony called **Sukhasan**. The reverse ceremony in a morning is called **Parkash karna**. Carrying the Guru Granth Sahib is a great honour. It is always held above the

*Reading the
Guru Granth Sahib
(notice the chauri)*

person's head. Sikhs respect the Guru Granth Sahib in this way because they believe it is the word of God.

Other holy books

No other holy book is as important for Sikhs as the Guru Granth Sahib, but there are other books which contain important Sikh writings. The Dasam Granth ('Book of the tenth Guru') contains hymns which were written by Guru Gobind Singh, some of which are used in Sikh worship. There are also books which help to explain parts of the Guru Granth Sahib. These are used when hymns are being explained as part of the service in a gurdwara.

New words

Gutka book containing the most important Sikh hymns

Hindu follower of the religion of Hinduism

Muslim follower of the religion of Islam

Parkash karna ceremony of returning the Guru Granth Sahib to the takht

Sukhasan ceremony of laying the Guru Granth Sahib to rest

Test yourself

What's the Adi Granth?

Who completed the Guru Granth Sahib?

What's a gutka?

Things to do

1 Explain why Sikhs treat the Guru Granth Sahib with such respect. Using the information here and on page 12, write down as many ways as you can in which Sikhs show their respect for it.

2 Why do some Sikhs have a gutka?

3 The Guru Granth Sahib is very unusual because it contains writings by people from other religions. What reasons can you think of why these might have been included?

4 Imagine that you have been asked to help to carry the Guru Granth Sahib in a Sukhasan or Parkash karna ceremony. Write a short article describing how you would feel.

Sikh Gurus I

This section tells you about the life of the first Sikh Guru.

The life of Guru Nanak

The first Guru of Sikhism was called Nanak. He was born in 1469 CE in a village in northern India called Talwindi. Today the town is called Nankana Sahib, in honour of the Guru. There are many stories about Nanak's birth and childhood which show that he was an unusual child, and he became a very religious young man.

Nanak's parents were Hindus, and Nanak was brought up to be a Hindu, too. When he grew up, he began work in a government office. Today, we would say that he was an accountant. The people in the office were Muslims, followers of the religion of Islam. Muslims have beliefs which are very different from the beliefs of Hindus. Nanak obviously enjoyed talking to people about their beliefs, and he learned a lot about the two religions. Nanak married when he was nineteen, and he and his wife had two sons. It seemed that his life had everything he could want.

One morning when he was about 30 years old, Nanak went to bathe in the river as usual. Then he disappeared. People searched for him for three days. When they could find no trace of him, it was thought that he must have drowned. Then he returned. The first thing he said was, 'There is neither Hindu nor Muslim'. This was very puzzling, but he told the people that whilst he was away he had been taken to see God. He had had a vision in which he had learned that just following a religion did not make people any different. Doing what the religion says – going on **pilgrimages** or making offerings – does not make a person religious. It is the way they live which really matters, and this comes from knowing God. Nanak said that he had been told by God to spend the rest of his life teaching people. A respected teacher of religion in India is called a guru, so, from this time on, Nanak was called Guru Nanak. He called himself Nanak Das, which means Nanak the slave of God.

The four journeys of Guru Nanak

Guru Nanak

One man who came to join the group was called Lehna. He became one of Guru Nanak's closest followers. Just before he died, in 1539, Guru Nanak said that Lehna was to be the next Guru. He gave him a new name, Angad, which means 'part of me'. Guru Angad was to carry on the work which Guru Nanak had begun.

New words

Meditate think deeply, especially about religion
Pilgrimage journey made for religious reasons

For the next 20 years, Guru Nanak travelled. He went to Varanasi, the holy city of Hindus, and to many other places in India. He went to Arabia and the Muslim holy city of Makkah, and to the countries that today are called Iraq, Tibet and Sri Lanka. Wherever he went, he told people that the way to find God was in the way they lived and what they believed.

At last, Guru Nanak settled in a village called Kartapur in northern India. A group of people who wanted to follow his teachings came to live nearby. They became the first Sikhs. 'Sikh' comes from a word which means 'someone who learns', and the people came to learn from the Guru. They met together to **meditate** in the morning and evening, listened to Guru Nanak preach, and joined in singing the hymns which the Guru had written. An important part of their life in Kartapur was that they often ate together. Free food was given to everyone, no matter what religion or social group they came from. In India at that time it was unheard of for people to eat like this, but Guru Nanak said that it was very important.

Test yourself

Where was Guru Nanak born?

What does 'Sikh' mean?

What does 'Angad' mean?

Things to do

1 Explain what Guru Nanak meant when he said, 'There is neither Hindu or Muslim'.

2 What was the name which Guru Nanak used for himself? What does this tell you about him?

3 What do you think Guru Nanak was saying when he gave Lehna the name 'Angad'?

4 Draw a series of pictures to illustrate the life of Guru Nanak.

Sikh Gurus II

This section tells you about the three Gurus who followed Guru Nanak.

After Guru Nanak there were nine other Gurus. Each one was chosen by the one before, and each one continued Guru Nanak's teaching. Sikhs believe that all the Gurus shared Guru Nanak's spirit. They say that the Gurus were like candles which have been lit from each other. All of the Gurus worked to develop the new faith. Some had to guide Sikhs through times of **persecution**, when they were punished and even killed for what they believed.

Guru Angad (1539–52)

The second Guru was Guru Angad. He was chosen by Guru Nanak himself. There is a Sikh story that he was chosen after Guru Nanak had set a test to see who should be the next Guru. He dropped a cup into a muddy ditch, and asked his two sons to get it for him. They both refused, because they thought it was not right for a Guru's son to do a servant's job. Angad jumped down into the ditch and fetched the cup without even being asked.

Guru Angad is remembered as being the Guru who worked out **gurmukhi** – the alphabet in which all the Sikh Scriptures are written. At the time of Guru Nanak, there was no agreed written form of Punjabi, the language which he spoke. People in those days were much more used to remembering things without writing them down, but Guru Angad made a collection of Guru Nanak's hymns, and obviously felt that it was important for them to be written down. Gurmukhi means 'from the mouth of the Guru'. Guru Angad also wrote some hymns himself. The name of Guru Nanak is mentioned in the last line of all of them. This is a way of showing that he was carrying on the teachings of Guru Nanak.

Guru Angad began providing education for young people, and encouraged them to learn gurmukhi. This was a way of helping to make sure that Sikhism continued. He also began building places where Sikhs could worship – gurdwaras.

Guru Amar Das (1552–74)

Guru Angad was only 48 when he died, and he chose a distant relative to be the next Guru. This man was Guru Amar Das, who continued the work of spreading the message of Sikhism. He stressed the importance of women preachers, and he was the first Guru to choose men and women to go out and preach to other people about the new faith. He began the custom of all Sikhs who could get there meeting twice a year at his home town of Goindwal. These meetings were at festival times. This meant that he could meet them all himself, and it was also important in keeping the new religion separate. Guru Amar Das also

The Guru Granth Sahib is written in gurmukhi

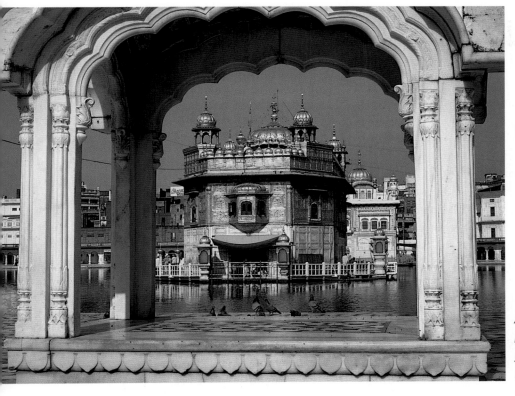

Amritsar, where building was started by Guru Ram Das

continued Guru Nanak's teaching about how important it was that everyone should be able to eat together. On one occasion, the Emperor came to see him, and the Guru insisted that he too should sit with everyone else and share the meal. The langar which all gurdwaras serve continues this teaching.

Guru Ram Das (1574–81)

Guru Ram Das was Guru Amar Das' son-in-law. He is remembered especially for writing the hymns which Sikhs use at weddings, and for beginning the buildings which became the Sikh city of Amritsar, in the Punjab.

New words

Gurmukhi written form of the Punjabi language
Persecution ill-treatment because of religion

Test yourself

What's persecution?

What did Guru Ram Das write?

Things to do

1 Explain how Guru Angad was chosen. What does this story tell you about Guru Angad's attitude?

2 Why did Guru Angad feel it was necessary to work out gurmukhi?

3 Why was it important for Sikhs to meet at Goindwal?

4 Imagine you were present when Guru Amar Das insisted that the Emperor ate the langar with everyone else. Work in pairs to make up a conversation between two people watching.

Sikh Gurus III

This section tells you about the later Gurus.

Guru Arjan (1581–1606)

Guru Arjan was the first Guru who was born a Sikh. He took over from his father, Guru Ram Das. Guru Arjan continued the building at Amritsar which his father had begun, and built a beautiful gurdwara in the middle of an artificial lake there. This gurdwara is now the Golden Temple, the most important building in the Sikh religion. Guru Arjan put together the Adi Granth (see page 14) and placed it in this building.

At this time, the Sikhs enjoyed good relations with the rulers of the country. However, in 1605 CE the Emperor of India died, and the new Emperor accused Guru Arjan of helping a rival for the throne. He was arrested, and tortured to death in 1606. This led to a change in the way Sikhs thought about themselves.

Guru Har Gobind (1606–44)

Guru Har Gobind became Guru after his father had been killed. He realized that the Sikhs needed to form an army if they were going to survive. They had to be able to defend themselves with force if it became necessary. He was Guru for nearly 40 years, and in that time he lived like a soldier, and worked hard to make sure that many Sikhs became excellent fighters. When he died in 1644, his grandson became the next Guru.

Guru Har Rai (1644–61)

Guru Har Rai worked to make the religion of Sikhism stronger. During his time, Sikhism spread more widely in northern India. He tried to make peace in the wars between the Sikhs and Muslims. Before he died, he chose his son to be the next Guru.

Guru Har Krishan (1661–64)

Guru Har Krishan was only five years old when he became Guru and he died when he was only eight. He is mainly remembered for the fact that he died of smallpox caught whilst he was caring for people who were suffering from the disease.

Guru Tegh Bahadur (1664–75)

Guru Tegh Bahadur was the son of Guru Har Gobind. Whilst he was Guru, the Sikhs were being persecuted again. Guru Tegh Bahadur was beheaded in 1675, because he refused to change his religion. (This story is told in more detail on page 30.) Sikhs remember him with pride because he was ready to give up his life, but not his faith.

Guru Gobind Singh (1675–1708)

Guru Gobind Singh became the tenth Guru when he was only nine years old. He is remembered as being the most important Guru after Guru Nanak. He began the **Khalsa** (see page 22) the 'brotherhood' of Sikhs who are full members of the religion. The special clothes which Sikhs wear, the five Ks, date from this time. Just before he died, Guru Gobind Singh said that he was not going to choose a new human Guru as the other Gurus had done. He said that in future the Guru would be the Sikh holy book. This contained the teachings of the Gurus, and it would be the Sikhs' only teacher. Since that time, it has been called the Guru Granth Sahib.

New word

Khalsa Sikhs who have taken amrit

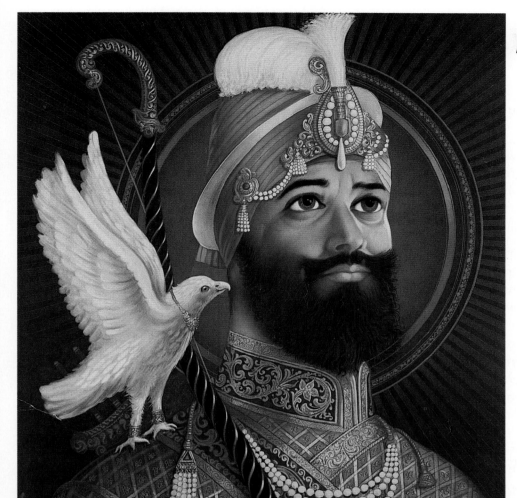

Guru Gobind Singh

Test yourself

Where's the Golden Temple?

Who was the tenth Guru?

What's the Khalsa?

Things to do

1 Explain why the death of Guru Arjan changed the way that Sikhs thought about themselves.

2 Why is the Golden Temple so important?

3 Why do you think Guru Gobind Singh is thought of as being the most important Guru after Guru Nanak?

4 Choose one of the Gurus mentioned in this unit or the previous one. Find out more about his life and work. (Encyclopaedias and books about India and Sikhism in the library will have information.) Put together a project with the information you collect, using suitable illustrations.

The Khalsa

This section tells you about the beginning of the Khalsa.

At the time of the tenth Guru, Guru Gobind Singh, the Sikhs were being persecuted and killed for what they believed. The Guru decided that they needed to form a fighting force which could defend the faith.

In 1699, Guru Gobind Singh called all the Sikhs to a meeting at Anandpur, in northern India. This took place at the spring festival of Baisakhi. When all the Sikhs were together, he told them that they needed to be strong to fight the people who were persecuting them. He asked if any of the Sikhs were willing to die for what they believed. No one answered. He repeated the question. Still no one answered. He asked a third time. At last, one man came forward. The Guru took him into his tent. There was a thud, and the Guru returned with a blood-stained sword. He asked the question again. Another man came forward, saying he was prepared to die, too. The same thing happened. Three more men were taken away, one by one. The people were terrified, thinking that the Guru had killed them all.

After the fifth time, the Guru went away. When he returned, all five men were with him! They were dressed in yellow robes like his own. Guru Gobind Singh told the people that because the men had been prepared to die for what they believed, they should be called the **panj piare** – the beloved ones. They would be the first members of a new group. It would be called the Khalsa, which means 'the pure ones'. Sikhs could only belong to this group if they were without fear, and ready to die for their faith.

When the people understood what the Guru wanted, many more men and women came forward to become members of the Khalsa. The Guru said that being part of the Khalsa was

These men are dressed to represent the panj piare

more important than anything else, so to show that they were all equal they had to do two things. One was to drink **amrit** from the same bowl. (In those days, people of different backgrounds were not allowed to eat or drink together.) Amrit is a special mixture of sugar and water which is stirred with a khanda, the two-edged sword. The second thing was to use the same name. This was a symbol that they were one family in the faith. Men were to take the name 'Singh', which means lion. Women were to take the name 'Kaur', which means princess. Since that time, all Sikhs have used these names as part of their own names.

Not all Sikhs today are members of the Khalsa. Some feel that they cannot keep the rules for living which it expects of them, and some do not feel that membership is important for them. Sikhs who do become members must be old enough to understand what it involves. Many do not join until they are middle aged. When a Sikh joins the Khalsa, there is a special ceremony called the **amrit ceremony**.

The amrit ceremony

The amrit ceremony must take place in front of the Guru Granth Sahib but it cannot take place in the worship room, which is open to anyone. Only Sikhs who have taken amrit may be present, apart from those who wish to join. Everyone wears the five Ks, and five Sikhs represent the panj piare. A sixth reads from the Guru Granth Sahib. One of the five beloved ones repeats the duties which members of the Khalsa must keep, and there are prayers and readings from the Guru Granth Sahib. Those who wish to join kneel in a special position resting on their right knee with the left one raised. This is a symbol that they are ready to defend their faith. Each person drinks some of the amrit, and it is sprinkled onto their eyes, hair and hands. After more prayers, the ceremony ends with everyone eating Karah parshad. When they have taken part in this ceremony, Sikhs are expected to keep all the rules and duties of their religion.

Washing the feet is part of the preparations for the amrit ceremony

New words

Amrit special mixture of sugar and water

Amrit ceremony ceremony in which people become members of the Khalsa

Panj piare 'beloved ones' – first members of the Khalsa

Test yourself

What does 'panj piare' mean?

What does 'Khalsa' mean?

What's amrit?

Things to do

1 Why do you think Guru Gobind Singh said that the first members of the Khalsa should be called the 'beloved ones'?

2 What two conditions did Guru Gobind Singh make for members of the Khalsa? Why do you think he did this?

3 Imagine you were one of the people watching when Guru Gobind Singh began the Khalsa. Write an entry for your diary describing the day.

4 Using the text and pictures to help you, write an account of what happens at an amrit ceremony.

Sikh history

This section tells you something about the history of Sikhism.

Sikhism was begun by Guru Nanak in the fifteenth century. He lived in the part of northern India which is called the Punjab, but he travelled all over India and to many other countries, talking to people about their religion. He became sure that God had a special message for him to pass on to other people. The message was that what religion you follow is not the most important thing. It is knowing God – what you believe and how you live your life – which is really important.

For 200 years after Guru Nanak's death, Sikhs were led by a succession of nine other Gurus. Whilst they were leaders, many changes were made as the new religion developed. Some of the most important changes were made by the tenth Guru, Guru Gobind Singh. He began the Khalsa, which really made Sikhism a separate religion, able to fight for its survival.

The Punjab

At the time of Guru Gobind Singh, Sikhs were being persecuted again for their beliefs. The rulers of the country tried to impose their own religion, and anyone who did not obey was punished. After Guru Gobind Singh's death, groups of Sikhs joined together to try to fight for their faith and for their own country. This meant that the persecution got worse, and for the next 100 years anyone who was known to be a Sikh was in danger of being killed. Many gurdwaras either closed or were cared for by Hindus, and many Sikhs began following their religion in secret and did not wear the five Ks or a turban.

Things began to improve for them when a young soldier called Ranjit Singh became a leader in the army. Battles were won, and he became the ruler of an empire which included the Punjab and much of northern India. He ruled for 40 years, and many Sikhs think of this as being a 'golden age' for Sikhs. However, other Sikhs point out that although he was a good ruler in many ways, Ranjit Singh did not

Ranjit Singh

country for Muslims. The border between Pakistan and India cut through the middle of the Punjab. Many Sikhs were bitterly disappointed. They had hoped that Sikhs would be given their own country. There were riots when Sikhs were forced to leave Pakistan, and thousands of people were killed. Many Sikhs would still like to create an independent Sikh country, which they would call Khalistan. In recent years, this has been the reason for much of the fighting which has taken place in India and the Punjab.

always follow the teachings of Sikhism himself (for example, he had several Hindu wives). Sikhs had freedom from persecution, but little was done to return to the teachings of the Gurus.

After the death of Ranjit Singh, the army became less powerful, and in 1849 the British took control of the Punjab as they increased their rule over India. There were treaties with Sikh leaders, and more freedom from persecution. Sikh leaders began to try to return to the 'pure' Sikhism which had been taught by the Gurus. There were still many struggles to keep Sikhism a separate religion, but in 1909 Sikhs in India won the right to hold their own marriage services rather than have weddings conducted by Hindu priests. This was a major victory, and it was followed by Acts of Parliament which returned control of gurdwaras to Sikhs.

Khalistan

When the British left India in 1947, the new country of Pakistan was created. It was to be a

Test yourself

Why were Sikhs persecuted?

How long did Ranjit Singh rule?

What would an independent Sikh country be called?

Things to do

1 Why did the persecution become worse after Guru Gobind Singh's death?

2 Explain why Ranjit Singh is so important in Sikh history.

3 Sikhs are often thought of as being excellent fighters. What do you think might explain this?

4 Use information from geography books to find out more about the Punjab. Why do you think it is an area which has been fought over so bitterly?

Holy places

This section tells you about the places which are most important for Sikhs.

Some religions expect their followers to go on pilgrimages – journeys to places which are particularly important for that religion. The Gurus were quite clear in their teaching about pilgrimage. They said that it is not necessary, because God is equally present everywhere. However, there are many places which Sikhs like to visit, usually because they are connected with events in Sikh history.

Amritsar

The most important building in the Sikh religion is the Golden Temple at Amritsar, in the Punjab. The temple is built on a platform 20 metres square, in the middle of an artificial lake. It was built with four entrances, as a symbol that people from all over the world are welcome there. In the nineteenth century, the Sikh ruler Ranjit Singh had the temple rebuilt in marble. The top half was then covered with gold leaf, and it was after this that it became known as the 'Golden Temple'. Its proper name is Harminder Sahib, which means 'temple of God'. The walls of the Golden Temple have verses from the Guru Granth Sahib carved on them, and the Temple contains very old hand-written copies of the Guru Granth Sahib. Readings from it begin at dawn, and the singing of hymns goes on until late at night every day in the Temple. There is a special procession every morning and night when the Guru Granth Sahib is carried to and from the worship room to the room where it spends the night. To take part in the procession is a great honour for Sikhs. Facing the Golden Temple opposite the main gateway is a building called the Akal Takht. This was built by the sixth Guru. Important meetings of Sikhs from all over the world are held there.

The Golden Temple at Amritsar

This gurdwara is at Anandpur

Nankana Sahib

Most important places for Sikhs are connected with the Gurus, and Nankana Sahib is the town where Guru Nanak grew up. It is now in Pakistan. It used to be called Talwindi, but its name was changed to honour the Guru. There are several gurdwaras there which were built to remind people of events in his life.

Anandpur

Anandpur is a town in a valley near the Himalaya mountains. It was there that the tenth Guru began the Khalsa. It is also the place where the head of Guru Tegh Bahadur was **cremated** after he had been beheaded for refusing to give up his faith.

Hazur Sahib

Hazur Sahib is a gurdwara in the town of Nander in southern India. It marks the place where Guru Gobind Singh died. There is a museum in the gurdwara where some of the Guru's clothes are kept. There is also a horse which is descended from the one which the Guru used to ride. This horse is used in the processions in the town which celebrate events in the lives of the Gurus.

New word

Cremate burn a body after death

Test yourself

Where is the Golden Temple?

What does 'Harminder Sahib' mean?

Why is Nankana Sahib important?

Things to do

1 What reasons can you think of why Guru Nanak said that Sikhs should not go on pilgrimages?

2 Explain why the Golden Temple has four entrances.

3 Why do you think it is a special honour for Sikhs to take part in the procession with the Guru Granth Sahib at the Golden Temple?

4 Make a poster called 'The Golden Temple' with information about it. Draw a picture to illustrate it.

Festivals I

This section tells you about festivals celebrating the Gurus' birthdays.

Gurpurbs

Sikhs do not attach a lot of importance to the actual date of festivals, and the celebrations are often held on the weekend which follows if this is more convenient.

Some of the most important Sikh festivals are those which celebrate the birth or death of one of the Gurus. They are called **gurpurbs**, which means a holy day in honour of the Guru. The most important part of a gurpurb is a reading of the Guru Granth Sahib from beginning to end without stopping. This is called an **Akhand Path**.

Akhand Path

An Akhand Path takes about 48 hours, and is timed so that it ends early in a morning. Where it is being read before a gurpurb, it is arranged so that it ends on the morning of the festival. The reading is done by any members of the local Sikh community who can read gurmukhi clearly and accurately. They take it in turns, reading for no more than two hours at a time. There is always a 'reserve' in case someone is ill, and the readers make sure that no break occurs, with a new reader taking his or her place behind the Guru Granth Sahib as the previous reader comes to the end of their section. The readers must bathe before going to the gurdwara, and immediately before beginning to read they wash their hands, so that they are clean to touch the pages of the Guru Granth Sahib. Whilst the Akhand Path is taking place, Sikhs make a special effort to go to the gurdwara, to listen and meditate. They try very hard to be there for the special ceremony which ends the reading. Langar is served throughout the Akhand Path, so a rota of volunteers is also needed to cook, serve and wash up.

Reading the Guru Granth Sahib all the way through is an important part of a gurpurb

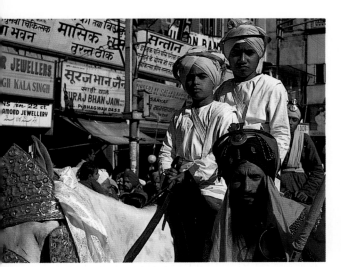

These two boys are taking part in a procession remembering Guru Gobind Singh

The birthday of Guru Nanak

Guru Nanak was born in 1469 CE, and Sikhs celebrate his birthday in November every year. This is the most important gurpurb, and is celebrated by Sikhs all over the world. The celebrations usually last for three days. In towns or cities where there are large numbers of Sikhs, there are processions through the streets. A procession is led by five people who represent the panj piare, the five men who were the first to join the Khalsa. Like the panj piare, they wear yellow robes, usually with a wide blue belt, and yellow turbans. Immediately behind them is a 'float' which is often beautifully decorated and carries the Guru Granth Sahib. The people in the procession follow, singing hymns which were written by Guru Nanak. Guru Nanak said that it was important for people to be able to eat and drink together, so people watching the procession are often given sweets or fruit and non-alcoholic drinks.

The birthday of Guru Gobind Singh

Guru Gobind Singh was the tenth Guru, and he was born in 1666 CE. His birthday is celebrated in December, and is the second most important gurpurb. Like the other gurpurbs, it is celebrated with processions. One of the most important is in the town of Patna in north-eastern India, which is where the Guru was born. There are also special games and sports competitions to celebrate the festival.

New words

Akhand Path non-stop reading of the Guru Granth Sahib
Gurpurb festival in honour of a Guru

Test yourself

What's a gurpurb?

How long does an Akhand Path take?

When was Guru Nanak born?

Things to do

1 Why do you think that the two most important gurpurbs are the birthdays of Guru Nanak and Guru Gobind Singh?

2 Think of as many reasons as you can why the Guru Granth Sahib is important in the celebrations of the gurpurbs.

3 Explain what an Akhand Path is. Why do you think Sikhs take so much care to make sure the reading goes smoothly?

4 Working in groups, put together a newspaper report describing a gurpurb procession. Draw a picture to illustrate your story.

Festivals II

This section tells you about gurpurbs which remember the deaths of two Gurus.

The death of Guru Arjan

Guru Arjan was the fifth Guru. His death is important because Sikhs think of him as the first Sikh **martyr**. A martyr is someone who dies for what they believe. Guru Arjan and the Sikhs became involved accidentally in a quarrel between the ruler of the country and a rival for the throne. The ruler ordered that Guru Arjan should be killed, and he was tortured to death.

Like other gurpurbs, Guru Arjan's death is remembered with processions. He was killed in the summer, when it is very hot in India, and part of his torture was that he was not allowed anything to drink. To remind people of his suffering, and as a sign of respect, people watching the processions are given non-alcoholic drinks.

This procession celebrates the martyrdom of Guru Tegh Bahadur

The death of Guru Tegh Bahadur

Guru Tegh Bahadur was the ninth Guru. He was also a martyr, and Sikhs are particularly proud of him because he gave his life on behalf of Hindus. At that time the rulers of that part of India were persecuting Sikhs and Hindus. The leaders of the Hindus came to Guru Tegh Bahadur for advice, because they knew he was a holy man. He agreed to speak to the Emperor on behalf of Hindus, and he encouraged both Sikhs and Hindus to stick to their faith. The Guru was arrested and taken to the city of Delhi. He was offered all sorts of rewards if he would change his religion, but he would not accept any of them. Then he was made to watch whilst three of his followers were tortured to death. Even this did not make him change his mind – he still said that it was important that everyone should be allowed to worship in the way they wanted. The rulers realized that they would not succeed in making Guru Tegh Bahadur change his religion, and ordered that he should be killed. His head was cut off.

Sikhs believe that the Guru's death shows an important lesson. He could have saved his own life by changing his religion, but he was acting on behalf of Hindus as well as Sikhs. If he had changed his mind, the persecution would have become worse, and they would have had to give up what they believed, too. He died so that people of a different religion could have freedom to worship as they wished. Sikhs say that this shows how brave he was. To die because you refuse to give up your own beliefs is very brave, to die to save someone else's beliefs is even braver.

The main gurpurb to remember Guru Tegh Bahadur's death is held in Delhi, the capital city

This gurdwara is built where Guru Tegh Bahadur was killed

of India, because this is where he was killed. There are processions through the streets, which end at a very beautiful gurdwara which is built over the place where he was beheaded. Then the people go to the gurdwara to worship.

New word

Martyr person who dies for what they believe

Test yourself

What's a martyr?

How was Guru Tegh Bahadur killed?

Things to do

1 Gurpurb celebrations often include giving food or drink to people watching the processions. How many reasons can you think of why this is so important?

2 Explain the different ways in which the ruler tried to persuade Guru Tegh Bahadur to change his religion. Why do you think he would not accept any of the rewards he was offered?

3 Why do Sikhs believe that Guru Tegh Bahadur's death was so brave?

4 Working in small groups, discuss the reasons why people might be prepared to die for what they believe. Think of some examples from people who have been in the news recently.

Festivals III

This section tells you about festivals called **melas**.

Sikhs celebrate two sorts of festival. Gurpurbs remember the birth or death of one of the Gurus. The other sort of festival is a called a mela, which means 'fair'. Melas are often similar to Hindu festivals, but Sikhs celebrate them in their own way.

Baisakhi

Baisakhi is the name of the first month of the year in the Sikh calendar. The festival of Baisakhi is held at the beginning of the month, and so includes the Sikh new year. In the Western calendar, Baisakhi falls on 13 or 14 April. It is celebrated by Sikhs all over the world.

The first Baisakhi took place in 1699 CE, and was the occasion when Guru Gobind Singh began the Khalsa (see page 22). The fact that

Baisakhi is the 'birthday' of the Khalsa means that today it is often a popular time for holding the amrit ceremony, the special ceremony held for people who wish to become full members of the Sikh religion.

At Baisakhi, there are celebrations at the gurdwara all day. The service begins soon after dawn, and lasts all morning, with people arriving and leaving, staying for as long as they can. The langar, the meal which is part of Sikh worship, is often served all day. There are readings from the Guru Granth Sahib, and poems which remind people of the first Baisakhi and how important the day is. Like the gurpurbs, there are processions with the Guru Granth Sahib being carried on a lorry or other open vehicle, and people singing religious songs. In many places in India there are fairs to celebrate Baisakhi. In the town of Amritsar, there is a famous market which is held every year, where farmers buy and sell all kinds of animals.

The Nishan Sahib is replaced at Baisakhi

Lighting candles for Divali

Hola Mohalla

Many other melas take place in particular towns or areas. The festival of Hola Mohalla is celebrated particularly in the town of Anandpur in India. This is the town where in 1680 CE the sixth Guru arranged a festival which took place at the same time as an important Hindu festival. This was a way of making people choose whether they were Sikhs or Hindus, because they could not celebrate both festivals. Today, there are sports events and music and poetry competitions, to remind Sikhs of the festival which the Guru began.

New word

Mela 'fair' – Sikh festival

An important part of Baisakhi is the changing of the coverings on the Nishan Sahib – the flag which flies outside every gurdwara. It is taken down, and the flagpole and flag are washed. A new flag may be used, and the yellow covers which are wrapped around the flagpole and the flag are always replaced.

Divali

'Divali' means 'festival of lights'. It takes place in November or early December. Its name comes from small clay lamps called divas. Sikhs remember it as the time when the sixth Guru was released from prison, and the people of Amritsar lit lamps in every house to welcome him home. Ever since this time, lights have been an important part of Sikh celebrations at Divali, and there are often bonfires and firework displays.

Test yourself

What's a mela?

What's a diva?

Things to do

1 Why do you think Sikhs wash and replace the Nishan Sahib?

2 Imagine you are a Sikh boy or girl celebrating Baisakhi. Write a letter to a friend telling them about the celebrations.

3 Explain why Guru Gobind Singh began the festival of Hola Mohalla.

4 Choose one festival in this section. Draw a picture to illustrate it.

Sikh life I

This section tells you something about what Sikhs believe about how they should live.

All Sikhs who are members of the Khalsa try to live their lives so that they are as much like the Gurus as possible. They believe that they should live honestly, and work hard for what they earn. They should care for other people, as the Gurus did, because this is the best way to worship God. Gambling and stealing are forbidden, and so is adultery (sexual relationships outside of marriage). Sikhs are expected to show respect for all living things. They do not have to be vegetarian, but no Sikh should eat meat from an animal which has been killed in a way they consider cruel. Most Sikhs do not eat beef. This comes from respect for Hindus, who believe that the cow is a sacred animal.

Equality

It is an important part of Sikh teaching that everyone is equal. God's love is for everyone, so no one is better than anyone else. They also say that you cannot love God if you do not care about others, because God made everyone. This explains why Sikh teaching says that men and women and people from different backgrounds should always be treated in the same way.

Sewa

Sewa is an important part of life as a Sikh. It means 'service' – helping others. The Guru Granth Sahib says 'there is no worship without good deeds'. The point of sewa is to worship God by helping others. For some Sikhs, this may mean giving money to help others. Guru Gobind Singh said that if they could, Sikhs should give a tenth of their income to help other people. However, Sikhs accept that this is not always possible. In any case, if someone has a lot of money, it may mean more if they give some of their time instead.

Sewa can take many forms. It may mean doing jobs like cleaning the gurdwara or helping to prepare or serve the langar, or caring for people who are ill. Often the jobs are things which people do not like doing. It is important to notice that sewa should not just be helping other Sikhs. Help should be offered to anyone who needs it, no matter who they are. An important part of sewa is talking to people about God, but Sikhs do not think that it is right to try to persuade people to become followers of Sikhism. Guru Nanak spent a lot of time talking to Hindus and Muslims, but he did not tell them they were wrong. What he did say was that what you believe is far more important than going through the ceremonies of a religion without really thinking about it.

Preparing and serving the langar is part of sewa

PEOPLE

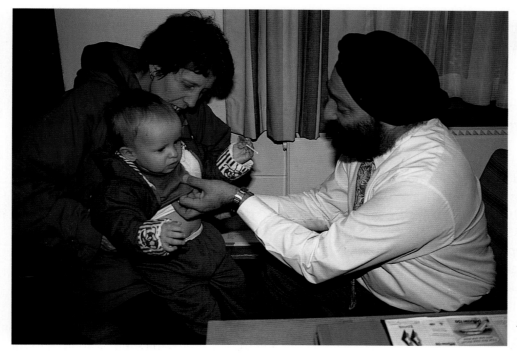

A Sikh doctor in Britain

Medical matters

Sikhs have always believed that it is important to care for people who are ill. There are stories about how Guru Nanak healed lepers – people who suffered from a dreadful skin disease which in those days had no cure, and of which people were very afraid. Many Sikhs today become doctors or nurses. In India, where medical care is frequently not available to people who are poor, there are sometimes clinics at gurdwaras, where people can be treated and given the drugs they need free of charge.

New word

Sewa 'service' – helping others

Test yourself

Why do most Sikhs not eat beef?

What's sewa?

Things to do

1 How many reasons can you think of why Sikhs might want to live like the Gurus?

2 Why do Sikhs believe that everyone should be treated equally?

3 Sewa – serving other people – is an important part of Sikh belief. Explain why they believe this, and give some examples of what it might involve.

4 Guru Nanak spent a lot of time talking to people of other religions. Write a short story showing why you think it may be important today for people of different religions to get to know each other.

Sikh life II

This section tells you about some ways in which Sikhs follow their religion in their lives.

Meditation

Sikhs are expected to spend time reading and thinking about the Gurus and their teachings. Thinking deeply about God is called meditation. Many Sikhs spend time every day meditating and repeating God's name. They also believe that reading the holy books is very important. The Guru Granth Sahib has been translated into other languages, but many Sikhs learn gurmukhi so that they can read it in the language in which it was first written. There are classes in the gurdwara to teach children gurmukhi.

Defending the religion

Guru Gobind Singh said that Sikhs should live their lives ready to defend their religion. This means they should not use anything which might make them less able to fight against things which are wrong if this becomes necessary. For this reason, Sikhs are not supposed to drink alcohol or smoke tobacco. They should not use any drugs except for medical reasons. Guru Gobind Singh also told Sikhs that they needed to be prepared to fight for what is right. Although Sikhs believe that violence is wrong, they also believe that if something is unjust, it needs putting right. If all peaceful ways have failed, fighting may be the only way. This is why one of the symbols of Sikhism is a sword.

Turbans

A turban is a piece of cloth about five metres long, which is wound tightly around the head and tucked in to keep it in place. At the time of Guru Gobind Singh, many important people in India wore turbans as a sign of power. The Guru wore one as a sign of the power of the Sikhs. His followers copied him, and this is one

There are classes at the gurdwara to teach gurmukhi

How to tie a turban

reason why many Sikh men wear turbans today. Some women wear turbans, but this is not as common. The turban has become an important symbol of the Sikh faith, and Sikhs should not wear anything else on their head.

In Britain and some other countries, there have been problems over the wearing of turbans. Uniforms which have caps or helmets need to be changed so that Sikhs can wear turbans instead. There were particular problems in Britain in 1972, when the government passed a law which said that anyone riding a motorcycle had to wear a crash helmet. For several years, Sikhs argued that this was a law which they could not obey. Some Sikhs felt that it was so important they chose to go to prison rather than give up their turbans. It took until 1976 for the law to be changed to give Sikhs the right to wear turbans instead of crash helmets. In 1989 a new Employment Act in Britain gave Sikhs the right to wear a turban instead of a hard hat on some building sites.

Test yourself

What's meditation?

How long is a turban?

Why did Guru Gobind Singh wear a turban?

Things to do

1 Why do you think many Sikhs learn gurmukhi so that they can read the Guru Granth Sahib in the language in which it was written?

2 Explain why Guru Gobind Singh taught that Sikhs should not drink alcohol or smoke.

3 How many reasons can you give why Sikh men wear turbans?

4 Work in pairs to discuss the rules which you think it is important to follow in life. Choose the five which you think are most important, and write about them, saying why you have chosen them.

The Sikh family

This section tells you something about the way Sikh families live.

Sikhs believe that family life is very important. They say that the best way for children to learn about the religion is for them to be taught about it at home. In India where Sikhism began, most people live in **extended families**. All the family – grandparents, aunts, uncles, cousins, as well as parents and children – live either in the same house or very close to each other. Brothers and sisters and cousins may be thought of in exactly the same way. The way in which parents and older people are treated is very important. They have had more experience of life, and so they should be respected.

In the past, Sikh parents often made important decisions on behalf of their children. This included choosing the person they should marry. This is called an **arranged marriage**. Marriage joins two families, so Sikhs feel that it is a decision which should be made by the families as well as the couple themselves. This means that everyone can be sure the partners are suitable. Arranged marriages are not usually as strict as they used to be. In the past, the couple never met until their wedding day. Today, young people often suggest a person they know, and the couple usually meet – though not alone – at least a few times. The marriage cannot take place if the couple do not agree to it. Many young Sikhs prefer to leave such an important decision to their parents, but it sometimes causes problems for Sikhs who have been brought up in Western countries. They see friends with boyfriends or girlfriends, and feel that they should be allowed to choose their partner freely, too.

Women in Sikhism

Sikhism began when Hinduism and Islam were the two main religions in India. Guru Nanak said that these two religions treated women as if they were not as good as men, and this was wrong. He said that even the most powerful man owes his life to his mother, so men should respect women. God is in women just as much as in men. From the beginning of Sikhism, Guru Nanak taught that women should be equal in every way.

A Sikh family in London

Women often lead worship in the gurdwara

There are stories in Sikh history about women who became soldiers and were as important as men in fighting battles for the religion. In worship, women have always been treated in exactly the same way as men. Women who wish to become full members of the Sikh community take part in the amrit ceremony, and they are expected to wear the five Ks, although many Sikh women do not wear a turban. In the gurdwara, women can take part in and lead services, and read from the Guru Granth Sahib. Men and women usually sit separately in the gurdwara, but this is because it is the custom in India in places where people are likely to be very close together. It is not part of the religion. Karah parshad and the langar are prepared and served by both men and women, and eaten together, and this helps to show that everyone is equal. Sikh women do not often take their name from their father or their husband, because they are always called Kaur. For example, a typical name for a Sikh woman might be Jasbinder Kaur or Surjit Kaur.

New words

Arranged marriage marriage in which partners are suggested or chosen by relatives

Extended family grandparents, cousins and other relatives living as one family

Test yourself

What's an extended family?

What's an arranged marriage?

What were the two main religions in India when Sikhism began?

Things to do

1 Explain what Sikhism teaches about family life.

2 What did Guru Nanak teach about women?

3 Give as many examples as you can from this section and anything else you have learned to show what Sikhism teaches about how men and women should be treated.

4 What do you think about having your marriage arranged by your parents? Write down three advantages and three disadvantages. Give reasons in each case.

Sikhs in Britain

This section tells you something about Sikhs in Britain.

There are about 400,000 Sikhs in Britain today, and more Sikhs live in Britain than anywhere else in the world except India. Many arrived during the 1950s, when people from many countries were encouraged to come to live in Britain. About two thirds of Sikhs now living in Britain were born here. There are many differences between life in the Punjab and life in Britain and some Sikhs find these differences quite difficult to accept. Most Sikhs feel at home in Britain, but they are very proud of their background, and do not want it to be ignored or forgotten.

Language

Many Sikhs now living in Britain are the children of British Sikhs, and have never been to India. They may not speak much Punjabi, and this can make it difficult to understand the religion fully. It can also make it difficult to follow services in the gurdwara. Some gurdwaras now hold at least some of their services in English, so that people who do not speak very good Punjabi can join in. Many children go to special classes at the gurdwara, so that they can learn Punjabi and gurmukhi.

Gurdwaras

Wherever there is a group of Sikhs, there will be a gurdwara. There are about 150 gurdwaras in Britain, but most were not specially built. Some are in houses or other buildings which Sikhs have bought and made into gurdwaras. In India, gurdwaras are usually open all day every day, and there is no particular day on which Sikhs are expected to go there. In Britain, it is often more convenient to hold services in the gurdwara on Sundays, because this fits into the British way of life. In Britain, weddings are

Most Sikhs feel at home in Britain

usually held in gurdwaras, although in India they are held in the open air. Many gurdwaras in Britain have also become important meeting places, especially for older Sikhs who have retired from work.

Converts

Sikhism as a religion does not now have **missionaries**. A missionary is someone who goes out to tell other people about their religion. Sikhs believe that their religion is the best for them, but they do not try to persuade other people to follow it. They accept that it is possible to find God in other religions, and believe that it is important to try to see God in every person. Guru Nanak preached to people of different religions, and welcomed them. Sikhism is a very open religion, and anyone is welcome to go to the gurdwara for a service and to share in the langar. Of course, everyone

Learning about other people's beliefs is important

who attends is expected to be respectful and take off their shoes, cover their head and make sure they are not carrying tobacco. The way in which Sikhs live has earned respect, and many people who were not born Sikhs have become interested in the religion. Some have decided that they want to live their lives following its teaching, and a number of people in Britain have now **converted** to Sikhism.

New words

Convert to become a member of a religion

Missionary someone who travels to tell other people about their religion

Test yourself

About how many Sikhs live in Britain?

When are most gurdwara services held in Britain?

Who can go to services in the gurdwara?

Things to do

1 Why do Sikhs in Britain go to the gurdwara to worship on a Sunday?

2 What reasons can you think of why gurdwaras have become important meeting places for Sikhs?

3 Explain what Sikhism teaches about other religions.

4 If possible, invite a Sikh to come and talk to your group about their life and their religion. Remember to prepare some questions!

Special occasions I

This section tells you about special things which happen to young Sikhs.

Birth

As soon as possible after a baby is born, someone repeats the **Mool Mantar**. This is the beginning of the Guru Granth Sahib and it sums up the most important things which Sikhs believe. It means that the first thing which a baby hears are the most important Sikh beliefs. Parents may share their joy at the birth by giving sweets or other small presents to friends and neighbours. It is the custom for relations to visit soon after the birth, and give presents for the baby.

The naming ceremony

The naming ceremony is often part of a normal service at the gurdwara. It usually takes place within a few weeks of the baby's birth, although it can be later. The parents take the baby to the gurdwara, and other relations meet there too. They are there to thank God for the

Parents often give a new cover for the Guru Granth Sahib at the naming ceremony

new baby, and to choose its name. (Many babies already have a 'pet name' which has been used before the official name is given.) It is the custom for parents to take with them a **rumala** (a length of cloth used for covering the Guru Granth Sahib when it is not being read) and to pay for the karah parshad which everyone shares at the end of the service.

At the end of the service, there is the usual prayer called the Ardas. When a baby is being welcomed, this prayer includes the names of the parents, and thanks God for the gift of the baby. At the end of the prayer, the parents go to the front of the gurdwara, and lay the baby on the floor in front of the Guru Granth Sahib. Then the Guru Granth Sahib is opened at random. This means that the granthi opens it without choosing a particular page. He or she reads the first new verse on the left hand page. Then he or she tells the parents which letter of the alphabet began the first word of the verse. The baby's name begins with this letter. For example, if the letter was J, it could be a name like Jaswinder or Jaswant or Jarnail. If the baby is a boy, he will also have the name Singh, if a girl she will have the name Kaur. When the parents have chosen the name, the granthi announces it to the congregation, and says, 'Jo bole so nihal' (this cannot really be translated into English). The congregation shouts 'Sat sri akal' (God is truth) to show their agreement. Then everyone shares the karah parshad and congratulates the new parents.

Sikhs often use the same first names for both boys and girls, so the name Singh or Kaur is often the only way of telling by their name whether a Sikh is male or female. Some Sikhs use Singh and Kaur as their surname, but others use their family name as well. For example, a Sikh man might be called Jarnail Singh Grewal.

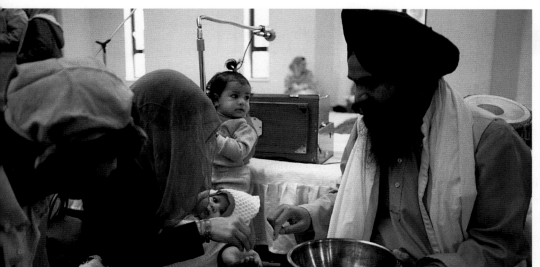

A naming ceremony

Sometimes, when the baby has been given its name, there is an extra ceremony in which the baby is given amrit. (This may already have taken place at home.) The granthi places a few drops of amrit on its tongue. The mother drinks the rest. Prayers are said, asking that the baby will have a long life, and asking God's blessing on him or her. The granthi may also give the baby its first kara – the steel bangle which is one of the five Ks. Tiny ones are made for babies, which are then replaced as the child grows.

New word

Mool Mantar beginning of the Guru Granth Sahib

Rumala cloth used for covering the Guru Granth Sahib

Test yourself

What's the Mool Mantar?

What's a rumala?

What's a kara?

Things to do

1 Why do you think that the Mool Mantar is repeated as soon as the baby is born?

2 What do new parents usually bring as a gift to the gurdwara? What reasons can you give why this custom has developed?

3 Imagine you had been to a Sikh naming ceremony. Write a letter to a friend, explaining what happened.

4 Look back at the section on the five Ks (pages 8–9). Why is a kara a suitable present for the granthi to give the baby?

Special occasions II

This section tells you about Sikh teachings on marriage.

Marriage

Sikhs are encouraged to marry, and marriage is called **anand karaj** which means 'the ceremony of happiness'. The Gurus taught that family life was very important, and being married is thought to be a necessary part of this. Many Sikh weddings are arranged marriages, and even if the couple have suggested their marriage the families will still be very involved. The bride should be at least 18, and it is usual for the groom to be older than the bride. A marriage cannot take place unless both the bride and groom agree to it.

Sikh weddings usually take place in the morning. They must always take place in the presence of the Guru Granth Sahib. In India, they may be held in the open air or in a marquee. In Britain they are usually held in the gurdwara. Any Sikh may perform the marriage ceremony, provided that he or she has been chosen by both families.

On the evening before the wedding, the bride's friends and female relatives may meet at her house. They have a party, where she is given money and special sweet foods. They paint beautiful patterns on her hands and feet with a special dye which will last for several days.

On the morning of the wedding, the bridegroom and his relatives are welcomed to the bride's house, where they are given refreshments. Often presents are exchanged, usually things like lengths of cloth for turbans or clothing. Then they all go to the gurdwara. The bridegroom usually wears a red or pink turban and has a scarf around his neck. He sits at the front, in front of the Guru Granth Sahib. The bride's father puts a garland of flowers on the Guru Granth Sahib. The bride enters, with her sister or other female relative. She wears red, often with beautiful gold jewellery. After bowing to the Guru Granth Sahib as usual, she sits next to the bridegroom, and is given a garland of flowers by her father.

The couple and their parents stand while prayers are said asking God's blessing on the marriage. A passage from the Guru Granth Sahib is read, and the person leading the service gives a talk about marriage and what it means. The couple are asked if they understand and accept their responsibilities to each other as husband and wife. When they have nodded their agreement, the bride's father gives her one end of the bridegroom's scarf. This is a

The bride and groom are given gifts of money

Readings from the Guru Granth Sahib are an important part of the wedding

symbol that they are being joined together as husband and wife. She holds it for the rest of the ceremony.

The most important part of the ceremony follows. This is the reading of the **Lavan**, a hymn written for weddings by Guru Ram Das. It has four verses, which are spoken one at a time, and then sung. Each verse explains something about marriage. As each verse is sung, the bride and groom walk in a clockwise direction around the Guru Granth Sahib. When they have done this for the fourth time, they are married. Everyone stands to join in the Ardas prayer, and there may be speeches before everyone shares the kara parshad. A meal follows, which may be held in the langar room.

Divorce

If a couple have problems in their marriage, both families will do their best to sort things out. If the marriage cannot be saved, divorce is allowed, and either person may marry again in the gurdwara.

New words

Anand karaj Sikh wedding ceremony
Lavan wedding hymn

Test yourself

What does 'anand karaj' mean?

When do Sikh weddings take place?

What's the Lavan?

Things to do

1 What does calling it 'ceremony of happiness' tell you about the Sikh attitude to marriage?

2 Why do you think Sikhs must marry in front of the Guru Granth Sahib?

3 When the bride holds the groom's scarf, what does it symbolize?

4 Design a card which would be suitable to send to a Sikh couple for their wedding.

5 Find out more about what the Lavan teaches about marriage. (Many books about Sikhism will have quotations from it.) Write your own version of what it teaches.

Special Occasions III

This section tells you about what happens when a Sikh dies.

Sikh teaching about death

Sikhs do not believe that death is the end. They believe in **reincarnation**. This is the belief that when you die your soul moves on to another body. This happens over and over again. Sikhs believe that they have lived other lives, in which they were not human beings, but they believe that only human beings are capable of knowing and loving God. Guru Nanak said that only reincarnation explains the unfairness of life, because the things you have done in a past life can follow you, to affect this life. This goes on until with God's help you become close enough to God to break out of the rebirth cycle. Then you will not be reborn, but will live with God for ever.

Sikhs say that death is no different from going to sleep. Just as you go to sleep when you are tired, and wake up ready for another day, so at the end of life you die and are reborn. Death is the end of one life, but the beginning of another one. They say that it is natural for people who are left to feel sorrow, but they should also remember that the person who has died has gone on to another life.

Sikh funerals

After a person has died, their body is washed by relatives of the same sex, and dressed in the five Ks. Then it is wrapped in a white sheet. A Sikh who has died is always cremated, which means their body is burned. In India, this takes place on the day of death, and the body is placed on a special **funeral pyre**, often on the bank of a river. In Britain, the funeral takes place as soon as possible after the death, and the body is taken to a **crematorium**. It is usual for male relatives to help to put the body in the incinerator, in the same way that in India they would help to lift it on to the funeral pyre.

The most important prayer at the funeral is the **Sohila**, which is the prayer said by every Sikh before they go to sleep at night. This helps to remind people that death is like sleep. After the body has been burned, the ashes are usually scattered on running water. This may be the sea or a river. Some British Sikhs have the ashes flown back to the Punjab so that they can be scattered there.

The funeral is often followed by a service at the gurdwara. This includes the singing of hymns, the Ardas prayer and the giving of karah parshad, as well as a langar. Sometimes there is an Akhand Path at the gurdwara, or there may be a reading of the Guru Granth Sahib all the way through at the home of the person who has died. This is done by the relatives and is called a Sadharan Path. It is not an Akhand Path

A Sikh funeral in Britain

because the readers will have to return to their normal jobs during the day, and so it is not non-stop. It is read early in the morning and in the evening. Sikhs believe that reading the Guru Granth Sahib like this gives comfort to the relatives of someone who has died.

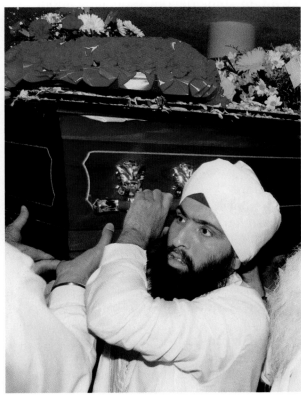

Male relatives help to carry the coffin

Sikhs do not put up any headstones or other memorials to people who have died. They believe that the good things which someone did during their life should be the way they are remembered, rather than memory of the person being based on a stone memorial. Stones are also forbidden to make sure that the memorial does not become a place for worship.

Test yourself

What's reincarnation?

What's cremation?

What's the Sohila?

What's a Sadharan Path?

Things to do

1 Explain why Guru Nanak said that reincarnation helps to make sense of life.

2 Why do Sikhs say that there is no reason to be unhappy when someone dies?

3 Explain why the Sohila is used at a Sikh funeral. If you can, try to find out some of the prayer.

4 Why do you think it is the custom for Sikh relatives to be very involved with preparing the body for a funeral?

5 Draw a picture or diagram to explain the idea of reincarnation. Think of some reasons why being reborn might be a good thing, and some reasons why it might be a bad thing.

New words

Crematorium place where bodies are burned after death

Funeral pyre special fire for burning a dead body

Reincarnation belief in rebirth after death

Sohila Sikh bedtime prayer

Glossary

Akhand Path non-stop reading of the Guru Granth Sahib

Amrit special mixture of sugar and water

Amrit ceremony ceremony in which people become members of the Khalsa

Anand karaj Sikh wedding ceremony

Ardas prayer which ends services

Arranged marriage marriage in which partners are suggested or chosen by relatives

Chauri special fan

Convert to become a member of a religion

Cremate burn a body after death

Crematorium place where bodies are burned after death

Disciple follower of a particular teacher

Eternal lasting for ever

Extended family grandparents, cousins and other relatives living as one family

Funeral pyre special fire for burning a dead body

Granthi person who leads services

Gurdwara Sikh place of worship

Gurmukhi written form of the Punjabi language

Gurpurb festival in honour of a Guru

Guru religious teacher (for Sikhs, one of 10 religious leaders)

Guru Granth Sahib Sikh holy book

Gutka book containing the most important Sikh hymns

Hindu follower of the religion of Hinduism

Karah parshad special food given out at the end of Sikh services

Khalsa Sikhs who have taken amrit

Khanda two-edged sword

Kirtan singing of hymns from the Guru Granth Sahib

Langar free meal which ends Sikh services

Lavan wedding hymn

Manji stool on which the Guru Granth Sahib is placed

Martyr person who dies for what they believe

Meditate think deeply, especially about religion

Mela 'fair' – Sikh festival

Missionary someone who travels to tell other people about their religion

Mool Mantar beginning of the Guru Granth Sahib

Muslim follower of the religion of Islam

Nishan Sahib Sikh flag

Panj piare 'beloved ones' – first members of the Khalsa

Parkash karna ceremony of returning the Guru Granth Sahib to the takht

Persecution ill-treatment because of religion

Pilgrimage journey made for religious reasons

Punjabi language spoken by most Sikhs

Ragi Sikh musician

Reincarnation belief in rebirth after death

Rumala cloth used for covering the Guru Granth Sahib

Satnam Sikh name for God

Scriptures holy books

Sewa 'service' – helping others

Sohila Sikh bedtime prayer

Sukhasan ceremony of laying the Guru Granth Sahib to rest

Takht 'throne' (for the Guru Granth Sahib)

Waheguru Sikh name for God